The *Witty* Guide to Wine

Text by : professor Tannin
Illustrations by : Gaël

Source

Layout : Dominique Gambier
Colours : Véronique Dorey
Translation : Roland Glasser

© Source Publishing, Genève 1999
ISBN : 288461 214 9

Y ou've had enough of fighting over the Coke with the kids ; maybe you're lacking in mineral salts ; perhaps you want to impress people ; possibly you're gambling on hoarding away some red gold or else your old nuclear bunker is in need of re-decoration. Whatever the reason, you have decided to invite a new companion to dine with you : some Fine Wine. However, although it may be easy to choose a Colombian herbal drink from the supermarket shelves, the wine section inevitably becomes transformed into a jungle of incomprehensible labels. And who would ever invite some stranger pic ked up in the street back home for dinner ?

Of course you could always get your loafers dirty in the mud of a vineyard or be smooth-talked by wine-growers eager to guard their secrets ; you could even read scholarly books, in tiny print and with no pictures, but that all takes far too long, and only hampers those who wish to get straight down to tasting. There is a quicker way... This guide, like its' subject, has been designed to give immediate pleasure to the wine-lover.

The œnologist is a barbarian who spits out his wine without drinking it. The drunkard is a barbarian who spits out his wine after drinking it. So let us remain amongst more civilised folk, guided by Bacchus and Epicurus !

Professor Tannin

Post-scriptum :
it goes without saying that this guide should
be consumed in moderation...

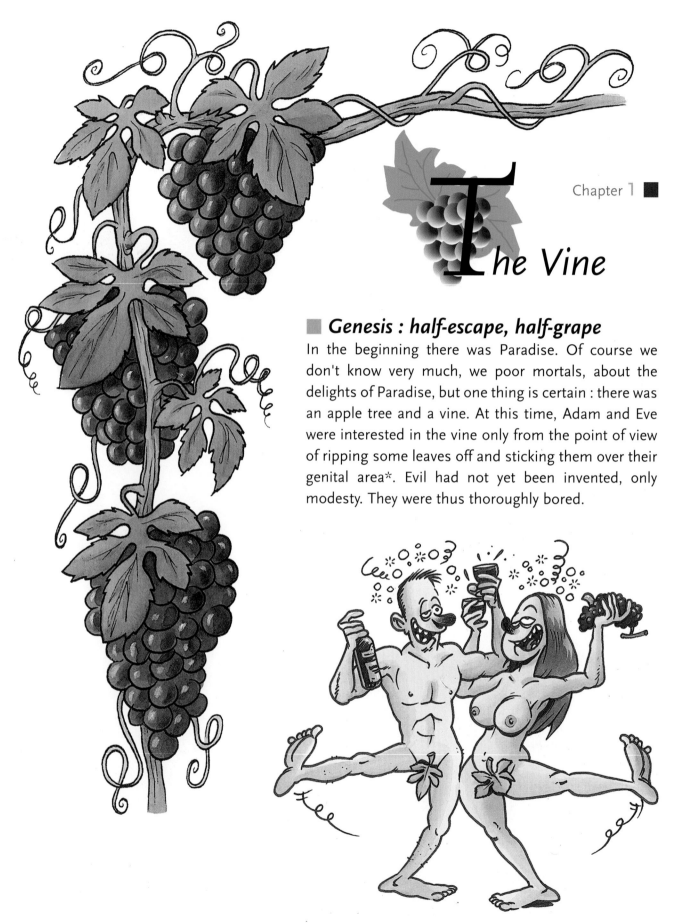

Chapter 1

The Vine

■ Genesis : half-escape, half-grape

In the beginning there was Paradise. Of course we don't know very much, we poor mortals, about the delights of Paradise, but one thing is certain : there was an apple tree and a vine. At this time, Adam and Eve were interested in the vine only from the point of view of ripping some leaves off and sticking them over their genital area*. Evil had not yet been invented, only modesty. They were thus thoroughly bored.

*The first mystery of humanity : how were these primitive G-strings fixed onto Adam and Eve's pubis ?
Since the vine leaf is not renowned for its self-adhesive qualities, theologians have become lost in their suppositions.
On the other hand, certain Soho hookers consider that the vine leaf was obviously not detached from its thick knotty stem.

Fortunately, there was the episode with the snake and the apple ; Adam and Eve were kicked out of Paradise and were obliged to find work. It was undoubted ly around this time that Eve invented the oldest profession in the world and Adam found refuge in the Lord's vineyards.

Ever since then, wine and carnal pleasure have been the founda tions of our civilisation. But although these fruity stories led to sin, for a long time the church was the only joint open on Sundays, ser ving communion wine. The sons and daughters of Adam and Eve are still sear ching for Paradise Lost, perhaps not in the form of the Garden of Eden, but of wine.

But where does wine come from?

Certain ancient books, tell us that it is possible to turn water into wine. That's going a bit too far, even if it is true that the grape is 95% water (but so is a human being ; try pressing one of them and you won't get a single drop of wine in your glass).

If the creation of wine is a miracle, it is also the fruit of one's labour, experience and passion.

So in the beginning there was the vine...

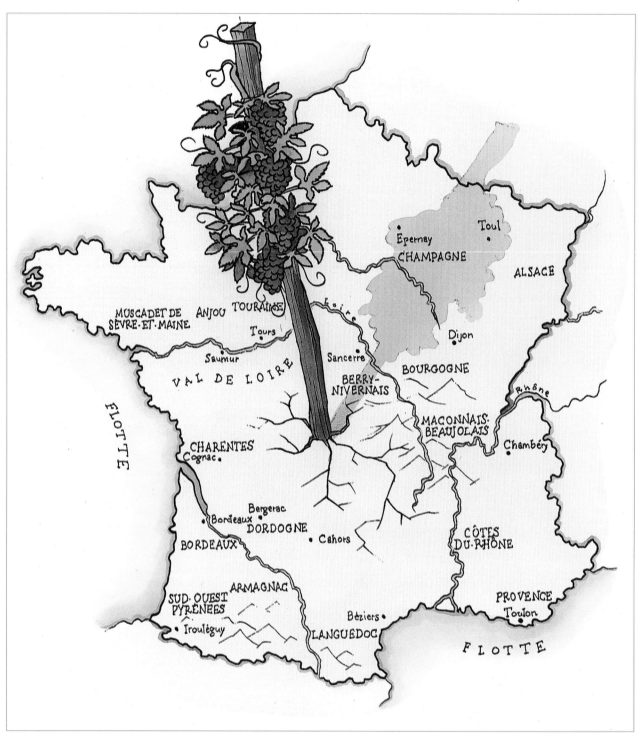

Map of French wines.
The hexagon has a blotchy face
but not a red nose.

◼ **Back to ze roots**

Learn everything about viniculture and add a rooty flavour to your conversation.

◼ **The vine**

Vitis Vinifera :

Botanical name of the common vine. Without it there would be nothing... except water and beer.

Cépages :

The particular name given to the numerous varieties of vine. E.g. : "in the vitis vinifera family I would like the Cabernet (or the Sauternes, or the Merlot, etc.)". But be careful not to confuse this with the site of production. The cépage is not a region. Don't say : "I am spending my holi days in the Merlot", and risk being taken for the lucky owner of a swimming-pool full of red wine.

Soil :

It is the ground which makes a good vine (see the wine map of France). Soil is not just a disgusting substance which sticks to your feet whenever you leave the path, it is also the source of all vegetable life. The vine is not an exception to this rule. However, since it is not very demanding, it can grow in poor quality soil. Soil which is not even good enough for wheat, costs more per square foot than an apartment on the Champs-Elysées.

BORDEAUX	SOUTH OF FRANCE	LOIRE VALLEY	BEAUJOLAIS
Le Semillon	Le grenache noir	Le Cabernet franc	Le Gamay

ALSACE	SOUTH AFRICA	AUSTRALIA	COLOMBIA
Le Gewurztraminer	Le chenin Blanc	La Syrah	Le Coca-Cola

Cep :

The base of the vine. Don't confuse "cèpes à la bordelaise" and "cep du bordelais". In the first case, the wine constitutes part of the dish, in the second case the wine is a long way from being in your glass.

Graft-stock :

A healthy trunk for a healthy mind. Without its graft of vitis vinifera, the graft-stock would be nothing more than a common stick planted in the ground. With its graft, it becomes the heal thy bearer of hardy and resistant roots.

Vine-shoot :

Young vine branch. Thou shalt protect it like a new-born baby. This is the wine grower's first commandment, their livelihood depends on it.

Vine leaf :

Primitive G-string stuffed with rice (Greek speciality).

Grape :

The fruit of all the wine-grower's labours. Cultivated and harvested with care, it will however, be trampled savagely in the darkness of a cellar. Wine is the vine's blood.

BANNED FROM THE BAR

The vine's enemies

Phylloxera :

Phylloxera : This insect is to the vine what the locust is to wheat and moss to green grass... except that the sly devil attacks the very roots of its victim. At the end of the 14th century, when Phylloxera munched its way through nearly all of the French vineyards, it was remarked that this little creature had succeeded in realising the dream of every tem perance league : the turning of

wine into water on French tables. Morality did not have the last word though. A vine shoot was developed that was resistant to Phylloxera, thanks to an American graft-stock ! Ever since, the Nappa Valley thinks that it is Bordeaux.

Mildew :

Caused by fungi, this disease specific to the vine is characterised by the rusty reddening of the leaves. The adventures of Tintin and Mildew are well known to the wine growers of Provence.

Frost :

Even more proof, if such were needed, of the perverse dangers of water.

The vine's friend

Wine grower :

Rich tiller of poor soil. His feet smell of his grapes but his wine never smells of his feet.

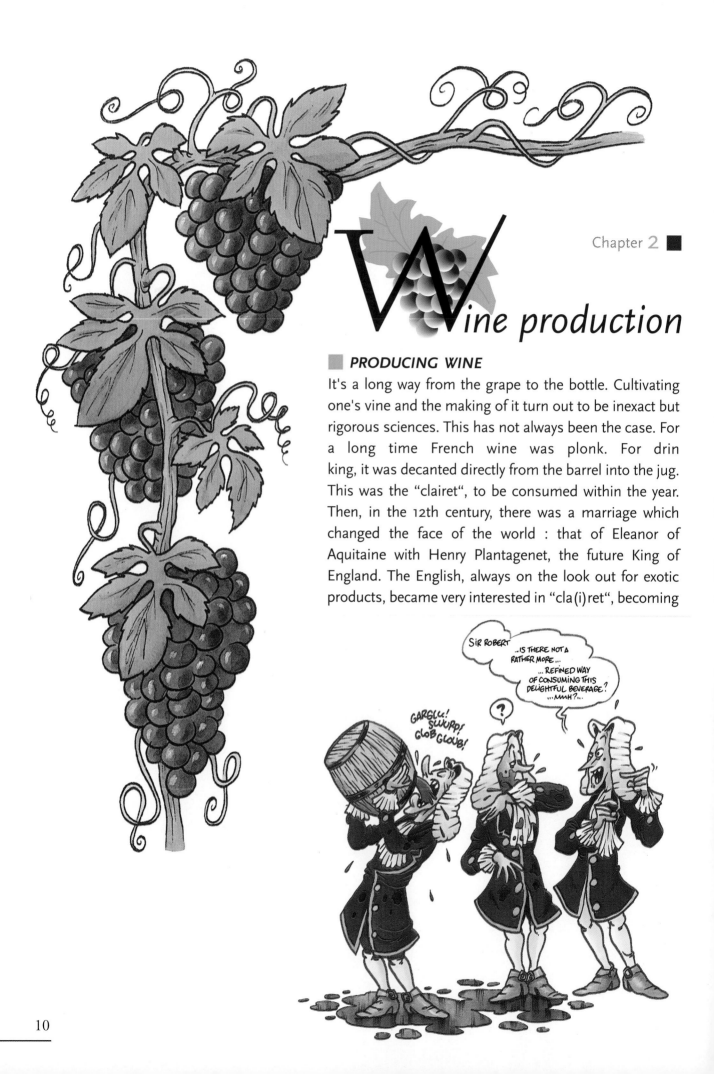

Wine production

■ PRODUCING WINE

It's a long way from the grape to the bottle. Cultivating one's vine and the making of it turn out to be inexact but rigorous sciences. This has not always been the case. For a long time French wine was plonk. For drinking, it was decanted directly from the barrel into the jug. This was the "clairet", to be consumed within the year. Then, in the 12th century, there was a marriage which changed the face of the world : that of Eleanor of Aquitaine with Henry Plantagenet, the future King of England. The English, always on the look out for exotic products, became very interested in "cla(i)ret", becoming the biggest importers of Bordeaux wine. Unfortunately, since their qualities changed quickly, these wines had to be sold and consumed quickly. It was not until the 19th century that clever London merchants sought to create more refined wines, the "new French clarets", bought young and destined to be kept for the long-term market. In the interest of increasing their profits, these English entrepreneurs came up with the idea of selling them bottled, corked and sealed, thus guaranteeing the wine's origin. Following hard on their heels, the French wine-growers concentrated their efforts on the quality of the product : choice of regions ("terroirs"), limited production, ageing in barrels and clarification of the wine by decanting. Thus, by the end of the 18th cen tury, the "terroir-château-grand vin" formula had been fully developed.

Today, with hindsight, we recognise that these Englishmen were the first merchants and consumers of "Bordeaux" wine.

HARVEST AND WINE PRODUCTION

From grape harvest to first fragrances, we follow the great wine adventure step by step...

Terroir :

It is the soil (terre) which gives the wine it's parti cular regional (terroir) flavour. For a wine's image, the "terroir" is the key marketing tool.
Be careful not to swallow any mud though.

Production :

No let-up for Vitis Vinifera. The fewer grapes pro duced by the vine then the better the wine. You have to work a lot to produce little ; another of the wine-grower's paradoxes...rich Lord of a field of pathetic soil... remember..?

Grape harvest :

The traditional image is of the annual bawdy festival which brings together German students, garish hippies and rutting wine growers. The reality is rather less exciting : exhausting working days, aching lower backs and sore fin gers, nights of comatose sleep, feet like watermelons. And at the end of it all, on the last night, comes the payoff : a great collective vomiting in the dormitory canteen.

Pressing :

In certain regions men plunge in right up to the waist in order to press the grapes. To make it easier they are completely naked. One hardly dares think about the origin of the bubbles which burst to the surface.

Grape-must :

As its name might suggest ('must' – Old English from Latin) this substance does not exactly inspire giddiness... no, this is simply the grape juice before fermentation. The tourist grape-picker will often find themselves tempted by the wine grower's favourite gag : grape-must tasting. Operation Laxative is thus guaranteed right through to the end of the grape harvest.

Fermentation :

The miracle that turns grape-must into wine. The scholar asleep inside me would tell you that this is due to the action of enzymes, secreted by micro-organisms... but that would demystify the subject...

Lees :

Rubbish tip. It is strongly advised not to drain the bottle right down to the lees, or else you're in for a rough landing from an otherwise quite delightful trip...

Decanting :

Ensuring that the lees remain at the bottom of the vat, the canny wine-grower decants the wine carefully into oak casks. (Try not to wear your favourite, newly cleaned white shirt whilst doing this...)

Cask :

To the eternal question "to beech or not to beech", the wine-growers have long since given their answer. The oak cask and the wine share a passion, a love which transcends... actually it's really just a mutual appreciation of each others' aroma.

Ullage :

Adding wine to the cask to compensate for evaporation. When one learns that the evaporated alcohol is called "the Angels' share", one isn't surprised at how they go about their work here on earth...

Tannin :

Preservative of vegetable origin. We find it in the grape and in the oak (still this crazy passion... sorry... mutual aroma-appreciation!).
This should not be confused with : Tannin (professor), preservative of vegetative origin.

Alcohol :

And all this work for what ? So that the fermentation of the sugars creates A.L.C.O.H.O.L! Between 8 and 14% by volume. The wine finally merits its name.

GLUG-GLUG, SNIFF

Body :

Characteristic of wine linked to its degree of alcohol. The less water that a wine contains, the more body it has. We can thus conclude that the more body a wine has the more it will go to one's head.

Robe (literally: 'dress') :

The colour. It dresses the body.

Aroma :

The subtle difference between "Hm ! this plonk smells alright !" and "What a delicious aroma of elderberries" (see list of examples on p. 14).
The size of one's nose obviously has no bearing on one's capacity for consumption.

Bouquet :

With several specific aromas we obtain a bouquet, the obscure alchemy of wine fermentation. Analysing the bouquet of a wine has become a distinguished international sport. You can try it in œnologist classes. It will be just like at the florists : you mix up all of the names, you remem ber only the price and if you knock it back, you'll still pass for a Philistine or Barbarian.

Examples of aromas to be thrown in to your conversation at random and which will make everyone believe that you have a good nose.

Spices, stewed fruit, blackcurrant, vine blossom, sloe, prune, vanilla, toasted, smoked and buttered bread, a hint of game, caramel, tar, raspberry, plum, butter cake, cinnamon, wooded, vegetable, liquorice, floral, leather, mushroom, cloves, peppery, grapefruit, cocoa, mandarin, menthol, choco late, coffee, lime-blossom, orange, grilled almonds, Morello cherries, hot stones, bread crust, crys tallised fruit, coconut, banana, pepper, carnation, cherry, fruit brandy, fur, tobacco, blackberry, blueberry, cardamom, eucalyptus, wild fruits, aroma, lily of the valley, strawberry, jam, spice bread, fruit drops, fruit salad, grenadine, buds, bigaroon etc.

(A test from Proffesor Tannin : There is an «odd one out». Have you found it ?)

EVENING DRESSES

The tastes and colours of wine are the subject of much discussion... at great length. To drag out your conversations, learn to conjugate the variations of red and white. (Colour-blind people should steer clear...)

Ruby, dark, purple reflec tions, fire, black silk, tran sparent, red currant, inten se crimson or with a cop per edge, garnet, orange ruby, crimson ruby, bright red, black-red, rosy, vermi lion, etc.

Chapter 3

Grading and designation

▨ FIRST CLASS AND STEERAGE

"When the wine is decanted, it must be drunk", according to popular wisdom. There are two possible readings of this statement. The first, and original, bears witness to an age when wine was still decanted directly from the barrel and thus its quality changed too quickly. This was the Middle-Ages, the age of plonk. The second, more contemporary, conveys the idea that if a bottle is open there is no question of leaving a single drop, down the hatch it goes... another one for the road and... hic ! In both cases the saying should be treated with caution, especially since it was probably spread by mercenary wine growers with the sole aim of getting rid of their surplus stock. After all, when the wine is decanted into bottles, one is not obliged to drink it... at least not straight away. Patience is one of the wine lover's virtues. Of course, not all wines merit such saintly patience. It's important to know the difference between a "Gut Rot" and a "vintage Saint-Emilion". The difference is just as important as that between cod roe and sturgeon roe. They look similar, but once they reach your palate, the first has become taramasalata and the second, caviar. Choose how to booze without losing your shoes!*

(This test-sentence, "© Professor Tannin", should be repeated 10 times after each tasting. Not so easy, eh... especially with a mouthful of Merlot...)

■ TO DRINK OR NOT TO DRINK, THAT IS THE QUESTION

Cellar wine :

No, this does not refer to your D.I.Y. vineyard under the stairs. It refers to wine which must absolutely not be drunk before a certain number of years have gone by, at any rate not without the agreement of the intransigent Vintage Vintners sect. You are thus condemned to drink without getting drunk.

Drinking wine :

These are new wines, local wines, from small or medium vineyards, which change quickly. To be drunk as soon as possible (finally some good news for our parched throats !). Ideal for eager D.I.Y. producers...

■ FOR INITIATES ONLY...

VQPRD :

No, this is not the abbreviation of some obscure political group (Very Quickly Proceed to Rabid Dictatorship) but one of the passwords which permit wine initiates to recognise each other : Vins de Qualité Produits dans une Région Déterminée (Quality Wines Produced in a Defined Region), It is official and controlled. In France it brings together AOC and AOVDQS.

AOC :

Even illiterates know what these three letters mean : Appellation d'Origine Contrôlée. It is the top class, that of all the "grands crus". The wine must have been pro duced following "the local, traditional and maintai ned customs", that is to say using the approved grape varieties planted in local ground and converted into wine according to the regional traditions. Grape production by hectare and the degree of alcohol are fixed by law and the wines are certified each year by a tasting commit tee. The word "contrôle" is thus not used in vain.

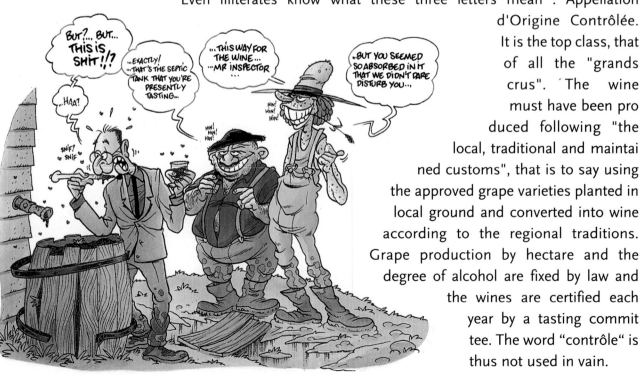

AOVDQS :

Appellations d'Origine Vins Délimités de Qualité Supérieure. Although different to the previous class it is more or less bound by the same rules. One notes, nevertheless, that the price of a bottle is inversely proportional to the number of letters in the abbreviation.

Cru :

Wine which comes from a specific vineyard or group of vineyards. Of course this term could apply to all wines, but the accomplished wine-lover, since 1855, has made it a qua lification of class : First, second, third and fourth grands crus ; Premier cru supérieur, Premiers et deuxièmes crus, Grands crus. But at the end of the day, when one drinks, the cru matters little, what is important is to get drunk ("NO, OUTRAGEOUS !!!" – Ed. – sorry folks, but the old editor's a leader of the temperance league... and this book is of purely agricultural interest and the publishers do not condone alcohol consumption of any kind... Thank you.) Moving swiftly on...

Millésime (vintage) :

Figure indicating the year of the grape harvest used to make the wine. With his obsession for storage, the accomplished wine-lover classes the vin tages accor ding to their conservation quality and not their drinking quality. This is certainly one of the steps in the plot hatched by the mil lenarian œnologues to prevent us from emp tying our cellars before the end of the world.

Vins de table and Vins de pays :

No man's land. Bottom end of the appellations and top end of the drinking wines. Here also there are controls : these wines come from more or less decent grape varie ties, the list of which is deter mined by law. In addition, their degree of alcohol is subject to rigorous monitoring (an inspec tor on the job is easily recogni- sed by his particular walk : he is the only one to adopt a zig zag path on his tour of duty. The good news is that these fresh, fruity and very drinkable wines are drunk young, IMMEDIATELY !

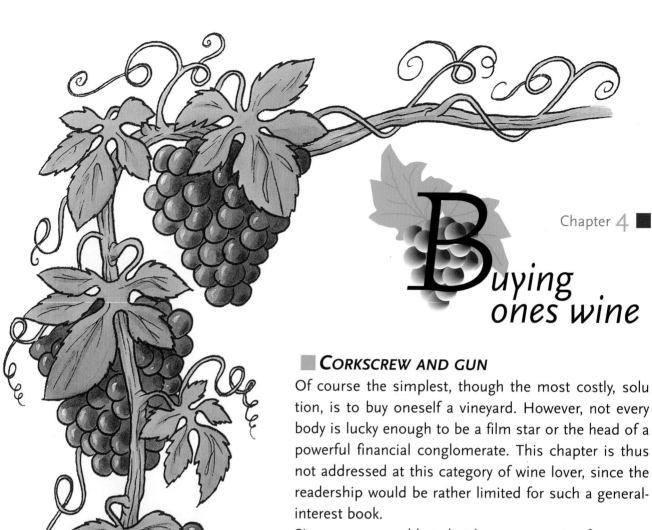

Chapter 4

Buying ones wine

■ CORKSCREW AND GUN

Of course the simplest, though the most costly, solution, is to buy oneself a vineyard. However, not everybody is lucky enough to be a film star or the head of a powerful financial conglomerate. This chapter is thus not addressed at this category of wine lover, since the readership would be rather limited for such a general-interest book.

Since you are unable to bottle your own wine from your own vine, you will have to become a hunter, since, just like big-game, stuffed-trophy hunter tracking the white elephant in the savannah, the wine lover, in order to satisfy his passion, must himself hunt down the perfect sublime bottle in the wine jungle. "Wines-R-Us Red" or "Gut Rot" can be bought in any 24 hour grocery store ; it looks like wine, it has the colour of wine, it gets you pissed like wine does, but bring home a bottle for dinner and it's just like whipping a rabbit out of your game-bag after a lion hunt. So as not to come home empty-handed, you must arm yourself with patience and a good corkscrew, know how to avoid false trails, outwit idiot traps, find your way through the maze of labels and, above all, never listen to your best mate, who always has a "nice little wine... off the back of a lorry" he can get hold of... (certainly not the best place to store wine, obviously). One last piece of advice : watch out for ambushes ! The wine merchant is also a hunter, but it is always the sucker that he has in his sights.

■ WHOLESALE OR HALF-BOTTLE ?

Wine in bulk :

Your best-mate's great idea, a 220 hectolitre tan ker of back-country wine, direct from the producer ! It's possible, but you'll be paddling in plonk. Then there is always the enjoyable, convivial and family activity : a holiday spent bottling and corking those 3,000 bottles which must absolutely be drunk by the end of the year ; permanent hangover guaranteed. If your best-mate is sensible, he'll content him self with getting you involved in the purchase of Cubitainers which contain no more than 20 litres... But even in this case, your best-mate will have taken you for a rather dodgy ride. The wine producer always selects the best vats for the wine that he bottles himself ; this commercialisation of lower-grade stuff is for bidden for the classed crus of Bordeaux. This wine, "sold for decan ting", is thus drawn from the ordinary and medium quality wines.

Bottled wine :

The simplest solution. You can find it everywhere, at the wine-produ cer's, at the co-operative's, at the wine merchant's and through the nor mal distribution channels. But why do things simply when you can make them complicated, your enlightened best-mate will retort. His cunning little plan that cannot fail, is to go direct to the source. Despite the undeniable privilege of shaking hands with the guys who press their feet on the wine that you will soon be pouring down your throat, you should realise that the produ cers and merchants are in agreement not to disho nestly compete with their distributors. That means not selling bottles for less than they do. Thus there are many Bordeaux châteaux which offer their products at even higher prices than those charged by the retailers. The declared goal is to dissuade those obstinate buyers who still persist, whether by ignorance, snobbism or stupidity (in the case of your best-mate don't delete any of the descriptions, they are all pertinent) in seeking cut price wine.

■ CHOOSING ONE'S DEALER

Sale of new vintage :

Remember the 1980's ! The name of the game was to buy anything in a large quantity (real estate, shares, cars etc.) and to sell it for a lot more immediatly after. It was the Golden Boy era. Wine has not escaped this strategy : the wine producer sells his product before having picked and bottled it. The interest for him, lies in having cash in advance (12 months). The interest for you, lies in buying the wine for a lot less than it would effectively be worth on the market (20 to 40%). Subscription = dodgy speculation ? Not necessarily. Remember the 80's... when the prices crash, the Golden Boy looks like a sucker.

Co-operative :

This union of small wine growers is the strong point of the wine growing co-operatives. It should not be confused with pro grammes in underdeveloped countries for digging wells and making pure water spout out of the ground.

Cellarman :

The man who knows the man who knows the vine. He is the specia list who will know how to balance your finan cial means and his need for cash. Contrary to popular belief, the cellarman is always prosperous and highly respected.

The wine club :

Armchair alternative. The clubs present a catalogue to their subscribers which contains a selection of wines drawn up by œnolo gists and distinguished French connoisseurs. Delivered in cartons or cases, the wine is sent direct to your doorstep. An elegant corkscrew in the shape of a vine-shoot is often delivered as a bonus. Doesn't that remind you of something ? Isn't that already how your best-mate buys his 120 piece tool-sets and his limited edition books (only 10,000 copies printed...) ? Of course, but "The wine club" is after all rather more chic than "Mail Order", isn't it ?

Wine bar :

How to make something new out of something old. Serving salami and cheese on bread with wine by the glass is a concept which already exis ted long before the invention of New Labour Brit-chic. We had our fair share of high-street Café de Paris, Dômes and Bistro Trendy's. We Anglo-Saxons, who have elevated exotic re-invention to an art-form, came up with a trendy version : the Wine Bar. The French, always on the lookout for revolutionary ideas, thus re-imported the concept back to the Hexagon, translating "Wine Bar" word for word, into "Bar à Vins". The only change was that it was possible to buy a glass of red after 11pm without having to order a snack on the side (Ah... the obscurities of British licensing laws...). And the benefit of this cross-Channel trip ? The cheese-chunk/glass of red combination has become chic and expensive.

Supermarket :

The only place which brings together all of the right conditions for rui ning wine : heat, light and noise. Nevertheless, since the recent public craze for quality wine, the big supermarket chains have seized this market niche. And so, during annual gastronomy-fairs, they open up their shelves to wine-growers, large and small; the rest of the time, it is not unusual for wine-sections to be run by real specialists. The resulting rapid and eclectic tur-nover has meant that buying bottles "on promotion", is much less of a lottery than it used to be.

Auction :

These are organised by an auctio-neer, assisted by an expert. It is vitally important to know the origin of the bottles. If they come from a big restaurant then it is probable that their conservation will have been perfect. On the other hand if they come from the "Cork and Bottle", that nice little pub under the dual-carriage way junction bridge, then watch it...

MOVE IT ON OUT !

Transport :

Wine is a delicate traveller. Some precautions are thus obligatory. The height of summer and the depths of winter are the least favourable periods for transporting wine, since extreme temperatures affect it permanently. For these reasons, wine is the drink of temperate climates. Moreover we can see how in order to overcome this terrible disadvantage, the Scandinavians invented vodka which doesn't freeze, and the Muslims in the South completely forbade the consumption of wine (of course, in North Africa, Moroccans and Algerians produce wine, but we all know that it is not they who drink it...)

Export :

Like everything which is produced in France, wine is subject to export tax. It is thus prudent to enquire about the import conditions for wine and alcohol in the country one is exporting to. The regulations may run from customs duty to import quotas, even to prohibition pure and simple. Smuggling wine is obviously not advised. We all know the technique of drug traffickers who hide capsules of illegal powder in their anus. But 5x2cm metal capsules are one thing ; a Jereboam (4-12 times the size of a normal bottle) is a completely different matter !

LEARNING TO READ (LABELS)

Obligatory comments :

Name of the cru, the type of appellation (AOC, VDQS, vin de pays, vin de table), degree of alcohol, the total volume, the name and address of the bottler. If you don't find any of these comments then you have just bought a bottle of grape juice.

Optional comments :

Geographical place of production, colour, type of wine (dry, mellow...), the year of harvest or the vintage, the grape variety, the wine grower's age, the bust-size of the decanting lady.

Selling points :

Means of production, certificates awarded, bottles numbered from one 1 to 80,000, Wine growers from father to son since 1974.

Corks :

Never trust the comments on corks. The only legal comments are on the cork-wrapper (the plastic thing which you screed up into a ball before uncorking the bottle and have just chucked in the ashtray...)

Chapter 5 ■

Storing one's wine

■ *THE CELLAR STRIKES BACK*

It is the wine lover's paradox : before serving one must save. Thanks to the enlightened advice of a specialist (not your best-mate ! See preceding chapter) you have acquired a certain number of bottles. Unlike a collection which starts as soon as you have two kinds of the same object, a pair of bottles is not sufficient to create a cellar. If you wish to avoid your inescapable best-mate's jibes – "You look a right mug with your cellar !" – then reckon on a minimum of twenty bottles. They take up room and will impose on him a minimum of respect as regards your credit rating... But that's the thing, it takes up space, which is exactly what your partner's response will be when you return from your tour of Burgundy : "You don't think that you're going to leave this mess in the middle of the kitchen ?" No, of course not. The kitchen is the environment least suited to the storage of your liquid treasure. Just like retired monks, wine needs to be left in peace in order to age. The vibrations from the dishwasher and washing-machine, the door slamming, the heat from the oven and other attacks are likely to cause irreversible damage to the quality of the precious beverage. Thus you no longer have any choice : to the CELLAR you go !

NO MORE SINGING IN THE BASEMENT

You live in a house or building and you are lucky enough to own a cellar : this rat-hole without windows, from which you emerge with your hands and face inevitably blackened with crypt-like dust. Up till now you have been using it to store your collection of rusty DIY tools, or shoeboxes filled with bits of string (they might always come in handy). If you hadn't had the generous but unfortunate idea of letting your children convert it into their rehearsal studio (wine hates rap and techno), then it would be easy for you to empty the place ("Oh No ! there's no question of you lea ving those old trowels and bits of string in the middle of the kitchenn !") so as to comfortably install the first protégés of your new hobby. And you will understand finally that this dark room, full of dust and spiders is the ideal wine cellar.

Darkness :

Wine fears light. Exactly the opposite of your best-mate who is not, unfortunately, himself enlightened. Thus the longer he stays exposed to the sun, the more his aspirin-coloured skin will redden. The wine itself is already red : its "robe" will pale under the action of rays of light. As for white wine, it goes without saying that you won't stain its "robe" with sunlight, a burst of heat however might well grant it a one-way ticket to the kitchen sink.

Smell :

A wine cellar is not a franchise of your DIY workshop. Corks breathe. If you don't want to permanently intoxicate your wines, remove from the cellar all the half-closed pots of paint, cans of petrol, fuel, oil, detergent, garden fertiliser... ("Darling ! What are those rusty, smelly old pots doing in the middle of the kitchen ?")

Hygrometry :

The quantity of water vapour contained in the air. Your cellar should be neither too dry nor too humid. Here again it is the cork which must be protected : it must neither get dry nor damp. Don't confuse this with hydrometry, another discipline concerning water, consisting of measuring the density of water (which might leave you thinking that what you took to be a humid cellar is quite simply a well !)

Temperature :

Temperate. The ideal is 12° centigrade. However, the temperature of your cellar may fluctuate between 8 and 18° without the quality of your wine suffering. The only exception to this rule : well frozen rosé. This practice is obviously considered a heresy by certain grumpy people but it's easy to see that they have never spent a long, hot and arduous day by the river with a rod in their hand, waiting for the trout to bite...

Ventilation :

This is the secret for an optimal control of both humidity and temperature. But be careful, above all no Force 4 gales ! This isn't the Round the World Yacht Race, nor the Common Cold research unit.

■ *GOING UP TO THE CELLAR*

Apartments with cellars are like flying fish, they don't constitute the majority of the species. And yet, you can't leave your cases and cartons in the kitchen for much longer.

("Hm, darling, is this a new recipe, mincemeat sorbet ?"

"Sorry, but I couldn't find the cooker behind all your cartons...".)

So where then ? The balcony ? Impossible to control the exterior tempe rature and humidity of a town of 400,000 inhabitants (or even a hamlet of just a few people), this is called meteorology and if it were possible to influence it, then Mr and Mrs Weatherman would no longer be seen on the small screen. So you really have to find a cellar in the enclosed space of your apartment, or if not, then in your loft.

Cupboard :

DIY option. Transform your cupboard by insulating it with glass wool or similar insulator, whilst equipping it with ventilation holes. The position of the cupboard is vital. Forget the one under the stairs (too many vibrations ; you might as well give your wine cases a good bash several times a day with a plank !) and the one next to the boiler (except if you wish to become the first amateur cellarman with an après-ski ambience in your dining room ; hot wine does have its follo wers...)

Commercial wine cellar :

Bank breaking option. It is a cupboard with controlled tempe rature and humidity, something which will really impress your best-mate. Ideal in a kitchen ("And the cooker darling, shall I put it on the balcony ?")

Professionnal storage :

"I wash my hands of it" option. Have one's wine stored by a cellarman. Advantage : you can forget all that you have read in this chapter, even the details concerning "humidity" ! Disadvantage : no possibility of uncorking a little bottle with your best-mate at 4 o'clock in the morning.

■ LAYING OUT THE TERRITORY

Space :

Ideally one should be able to classify all the wines by region while still being able to keep a space for new acquisitions. A spacious cellar allows you to keep your wines in the best condition. The well being of your wine depends upon the size of your cellar. As Stanley Kubrick once said : "The only luxury is space."

Racks :

Only Magnums (twice the size of a normal bottle) may be kept in their original cases. Racks are thus indispensable for organising your standard bottles. With the aid of your best-mate, you can make them yourself in metal, wood or polystyrene. Adjustable, they should have a minimum depth of 30cm and a width equivalent to 2 dozen bottles. If you are frightened by the idea of passing a day next to your clumsy best-mate armed with a saw and a drill, there is an even more simple answer : buy prefabricated, interlocking racks. At this point along the expenditure route, the credit-rating commission company will not make a fuss about such a small sum.

Organisation :

The layout of a cellar must be as rigorous as that of a library. One doesn't mix up the classics of Noh theatre with "The Adventures of Tin-Tin".
From top to bottom :

- long-term cellar red
- cellar red
- red to be drunk soon
- rosé
- dry white
- cellar white (mellow and syrupy)

Don't wait until you have put away all of your bottles to remind yourself that logically, their labels should be turned upwards and the neck of the bottle towards you (otherwise, it's as if you put away all of your library books the wrong way round...)

■ FIRST AID KIT

It's three o'clock in the morning and you are suddenly awoken by the piercing cry of a bottle of wine in the cellar. Nightmare, fore sight or delirium tremens, it doesn't matter, you must act quickly and ease the crisis by opening the bottle concerned. But are you sufficiently equipped ?

Thermometer :

Intended for taking the temperature of your cellar. Often much bigger than a medical thermometer, so avoid sticking it in the wrong place.

Hygrometer :

Not to be confused with "hydrometer", our little liquid-density measu ring friend that we came across before; it would be rather worrying as far as your cellar's humidity was concerned, if you had one of these in there...

Corkscrew :

The only truly dangerous object in your cellar. You would do well to avoid sitting on it.

Carafe:

For decanting. Without it you risk being left high and dry.

Ice bucket :

For cooling the wine.

Thermometer :

This one is for measuring the temperature of the wine. The rumour that it might be confused with its medical equivalent, remains bottomless.

Corks :

If your best-mate isn't there to help you finish off the bottles, you will have to re-cork them. Leave plastic stoppers for vinegar and use conical corks, the easiest ones to manipulate without a corking device or corkscrew.

The wine glass :

You are not going to drink directly from the bottle nor use a plastic or metal cup. A wine glass is to the wine bottle what a trunk is to an elephant : an extension.

Cellar book :

The only book sold with white pages which you must blacken yourself. In the log book of your wine producing slave-galley, you should write down : name of the wine, year, region, type of wine, grape variety, pre sumed peak, maximum conservation, to be drunk from the following date..., position in the cellar, supplier's address, quantity bought, order date, delivery date, bottle price, total price, consumption date, number of bottles opened... and... remaining, food served, tasting notes and comments (except those of your best mate, of course).

■ *"BOTTLED BY THE BUYER"*

You have not been able to resist the idea of bringing a bottle bearing the explicit label "bottled by buyer" to the next meal with your best mate. You have kept a cool head and avoided the 220 hectolitre tanker, nevertheless there you are with a 40 litre Cubitainer on your hands, and it's heavy ! Obviously there is no question of emptying it according to your needs, unless you have decided to stock enough vinegar to season several thousand salads. If the wine has been transported in a Cubitainer, it must be bottled quickly. If it is in a barrel, it must definitely be left to rest for a fortnight. In any event, you should choose a day when the weather is clement : high pressure without rain or storm (it is no longer a wine guide that you require, but a weather forecast...).

Bottle :
Shaped according to the wine (see picture), clean and dry.

LEARNING HOW TO DISTINGUISH BETWEEN BOTTLES.

1. Bordeaux bottles often contain cellar-wine. They are thus recognisable by their broad shoulders which have to catch and hold the deposits.

2 Tall and bulging bottles are typical of Provence, and can hold white as well as red or rosé...

3. Short and squat, with slouching shoulders, the Burgundy bottle has been adopted all over the world...

4 In Germany, they like them tall and svelte. This long and slim bottle is ideal for white wines...

Wine funnel :

Pour the wine down the inside surface of the bottle, keeping the bottle slightly tilted, so as to limit mixing and oxidisation (especially for white wines). Under no circumstances should a froth appear at the surface of the liquid : don't shake the bottle-filler during use...

Cork :

Made out of cork (as opposed to plastic !), 6mm longer than the bottle's neck. Several schools of thought promote distinct cork-softening techniques. Some recommend plunging them into cold water for several hours, others into very hot water for ten minutes.

A last school recommends softening in tepid water. All rather confusing really...

Corker :

One of your best-mate's girlfriends.

Label :

Identity card. Here also, concerning the adhesion of the label, there are several schools of thought : wallpaper paste (ideal for handing down to your great-grandchildren - totally irremovable labels), water and flour mix (several years of peace) or the water and milk mix (several hours of adhesion).

Demand from your supplier, labels on which it is expressly written that this wine has been "bottled by the buyer", because otherwise, what's the point of going to so much trouble ?!

Chapter 6

The pleasure of wine

■ AT LAST WE DRINK !

One can safely say that if you had chosen to indulge a passion for lemonade or long-life milk, you would not have been obliged to digest five chapters, intended to quench your thirst for wine knowledge, and then wait for the sixth one in order to hear, finally, the melodious sound of the bottle uncorking – "Plop !"

It is what we call a rite of passage because, as you have now understood, wine is an initiates' club.
But not a closed club, more like a convivial network.
With this new chapter, your crossing of the desert

comes to a close. After having made your mouth water, it's time to get to the heart of the matter and proceed with the tasting.

It remains only for you to sacrifice yourself to the initiatory tasting rites, accompanied by a classical choir booming :

"Knees Up Mother Brown"

TASTING

One doesn't open a good bottle of wine on the tailgate of the delivery lorry. A tasting cannot take place anywhere, anytime or anyhow. All rituals need certain formality (No, no, it doesn't mean top-hat and tails...)

The peak :

This is not the maximum longevity before turning to vinegar, it is the moment when the wine will give you the best of itself. Before this time it is not the right time, and after time you're just a speculator.

A few pointers for calculating the approximate peak of a wine

- Alsace : within the year.
- Alsace grand cru : 1-4.
- Alsace late grape harvest : 8-12.
- Jura : 4 (white), 8 (red).
- Jura rosé : 6.
- Yellow wine : 20.
- Savoie : 1-2 (white); 2-4 (red).
- Bourgogne : 5 (white), 7 (red).
- Grand Bourgogne : 5-10 (white), 10-15 (red).
- Mâcon : 2-3 (white), 1-2 (red).
- Beaujolais : within the year.
- Cru du Beaujolais : 1-4.
- Coca-Soda : 144-200 (light years).
- Valley of the North Rhône : 2-3 (white); 4-5 (red).
- Valley of the Southern Rhône : 2 (white); 4-8 (red).
- Loire : 5-10 (white), 5-12 (red).
- Mellow, syrupy Loire : 10-15.
- Bordeaux : 2-3 (white), 6-8 (red).

- Gut Rot : 2 days (European blend).
- Grand Bordeaux : 8-10 (white), 10-15 (red).
- Syrupy Bordeaux : 10-15.
- Cahors : 9-10.
- Languedoc : 1-2 (white), 2-4 (red).
- Côtes de Provence : 1-2 (white), 2-4 (red).
- Corse : 1-2 (white), 2-4 (red).

(An interloper has slipped into the table, which you will certainly have already picked up on and thrown down the sink...).

WELL... it's CERTAINLY TRUE THAT WITHOUT A GLASS...

... IT IMMEDIATELY STARTS TO LOSE A BIT OF ITS CHARM !!

siiiOOURPPPPP!

Location :

There is certainly little risk that you will be forced to open your bottle in a walk-in fridge or next to the furnace of a steam loco motive. But between these two extremes, you should remain temperate (I didn't say "sober") : from 18-20°C. It is obvious that here, more than ever, one should avoid any unwelcome smells. Ask your best-mate to extinguish his cigarette but, above all, stop him from covering himself with cheap after-shave which fouls up your taste-buds. Following the same line of advice, stay away from night-club laser shows ; a wine with an orange "robe" loses much of its visual interest.

Glass :

Natural extension of the hand. It's better to clean one's teeth in a foot-bath than to clean one's feet in a tooth-mug. It's the same for wine.

■ TANTALUS'S TORMENT (WHEN TO UNCORK ?)

Can we push the cork further in this mental torture ? Yes. The "plop" of its liberation still sounds in your ears and you can already hear the wine pouring down your throat "glug glug". But no ! Not so quick ! Not all wines are so neatly deflowered on the corner of the kitchen table...

- **Aromatic white wines, wines of the latest vintage, current wines, rosé wines :** uncork, drink without delay. Keep the bottle vertical.
- **Loire white wines, syrupy white wines :** uncork, wait for an hour. Keep the bottle vertical.
- **Young red wines, red wines at their peak :** decant half-an hour to two hours before consumption.
- **Delicate old red wines :** uncork in a pouring basket, and serve without delay : possibly decant and drink straight away.
- **Gut Rot wines :** uncork, empty out onto some kindling and strike a match. Your barbecue is now lit.

This is it. The bottle is there in front of you, uncorked. Your glass is full. That of your best-mate's also. "It's time to sling it down the hatch !" remarks your impatient buddy who always wears the same Man United triple-cup winners T-shirt. Your best-mate evidently takes himself for an all-round champion). And this lout then turns word into deed. He slings down the delicate potion like a soldier just back from the war. In one go. Sacrilege ! It's time that you gave him a lesson in the finer points of drinking.

Serving temperature :

It's possible to kill a wine by serving it at an unsuitable temperature, or, on the other hand, enhance it by serving it at the appropriate temperature. The wine thermometer is thus indispensable (that which you best-mate has just confused with a medical thermometer...).

- **Great Bordeaux red wines :** 16-17°.
- **Great Burgundy red wines :** 15-16°.
- **Quality red wines, great red wines before their peak :** 14-16°.
- **Great dry white wines :** 14-16°.
- **Light, fruity, young red wines :** 11-12°.
- **Rosé wines, wines of the latest vintage :** 10-12°.
- **Dry white wines, red vin de pays :** 10-12°.
- **Little whites, white vin de pays :** 8-10°.
- **Champagne, sparkling :** 7-8°.
- **Syrupy :** 6°.
- **Mulled cinnamon wine :** 40°.

IDENTIFICATION OF DESIRE

Just like making love, tasting requires the senses of sight, smell, taste and touch...

The Eye :

The first contact with the wine is visual : we look for the secrets hidden under its dress. The examination is carried out by holding the glass between the eye and a light source placed at the same height ; a basic principle of strip-tease, your best friend will tell you. Whatever the colour and tint, the 'robe' must be clear and undisturbed. Observing it will tell you the age of the wine and its state of conservation. The more transparent it is, the younger it is... Again using ones eye (isn't vision great...), we can observe the "legs", those rivulets which the wine forms on the side of the glass when one moves it with a swirling motion to sniff the bouquet. We can thus determine its degree of alcohol. Be careful : the more the "legs" stick to the glass, the more they will go to your head. Look but don't touch.

... WHAT AN IDEA! DISGUISING YOURSELF AS CARLSBERG AT AN OENOLOGUES PARTY!

I MEAN REALLY!

The nose :

Now, you can stick your nose under the dress. You will start by sniffing the perfumes given off from the glass by setting the wine moving in rotation. You must get a good whiff in your nose, so your wrist action needs to be good. (Remember : wine stains ! Before swirling glasses in public, train yourself properly in the bath). The quality of a wine depends on the intensity and complexity of the bouquet. Thus, the great wines are characterised by ample and deep bouquets... The others can be described in one word... Since the vocabulary relative to the bouquet proceeds by analogy (see chapter 3), it is, by nature, infinite. Having arrived at this point in the tasting, and if your public consists of hand-picked friends (who know nothing), you can thus say whatever you like, using choice and poetic words like : "This bouquet smells of prawns".

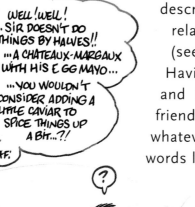

WELL ! WELL ! ... SIR DOESN'T DO THINGS BY HALVES !! ... A CHATEAUX-MARGAUX WITH HIS EGG MAYO... ... YOU WOULDN'T CONSIDER ADDING A LITTLE CAVIAR TO SPICE THINGS UP A BIT...?!

PF !

The mouth :

This is the moment. You can let the wine slide between your mouth and your palette. And no, we don't swallow straight away, a little more patience please. So as to allow the bouquet to spread fully through the oral cavity, you will first breathe in a little air (without gargling or gurgling). Since the taste-buds on the tongue are sensitive only to the four basic tastes – bitter, acidic, sweet, sour – it is via the retro-nasal passage that the wine spreads new aromatic elements (redro-nasal package for those with a cold !). Here again, you should not lack words to express your joy or disappointment. From now on you know who you're dealing with...

Critical : unformed, soft, flat, thin, watery, limited, transparent, poor, heavy, massive, ugly, thick, cat's piss...

Laudatory : structured, constructed, powerfully built, well rounded, full, elegant, fine, rich, balanced... seeking some company for an evening... or maybe for life...

■ NOW, FINALLY, YOU MAY SWALLOW...

"This is the moment carefully chosen by your best-mate to give you a big slap on the back" – "Not a bad little plonk you got there, me old chap !"
Due to the thump received, you immediately spit out this first mouthful that you have been keenly anticipating for the last six chapters !
"It's a pity to waste all this good plonk", your best-mate remarks.

At this stage, you can close this book and recommence the entire operation on your own...

Post-Script
And the next day ?

Aspirin :
Miracle of science
designed to render
your hangover... over...

Chapter 7

Wine atlas

Explore the vineyards of France, accompanied by Professor Tannin, without ever leaving your armchair.

One of my eminent colleagues, Professor Theodore Monod, the explorer, liked to explain how nothing more than a simple road map was enough to evoke old voyages and new lands to explore. This atlas of French wines will thus be dedicated to all those Theodore Monods slumbering within you ...

INSTRUCTIONS FOR USE

Each wine-producing region has it wine map. Each wine has its notes. These notes are in two parts. First of all the average time it should be kept for. Secondly, for the gourmet, the most appropriate accompaniment.

A few preliminary culinary tips, just to help you find your way :

- Wine does not go well with vinaigrette, chocolate or coffee flavoured desserts, certain strong tasting herbs and plants like mint, cress, sorrel, artichoke, asparagus. These are the only times when you will be obliged to serve water (OK... we won't start this again... promise !)

- No fine wine with spicy dishes, but rather a chilled wine, rosé or a young, dry white (stock up).

- A dish cooked with wine should be served with a wine from the same region.

- The sweeter the dessert, the drier the wine should be.

- Old customs are not necessarily Golden Rules : so with fish you can open a light Loire or a chilled rosé.

- If two red wines are served during the same meal, it would be preferable if they came from the same region.

- Loosen your belts, rinse your glasses...
let's hit the road...

Wines of Bordeaux

Barsac
4 to 25 years.
Foie gras, fish, desserts.

Blaye
4 to 6 years.
Seafood

Bordeaux
2 to 3 years.
Bonne bouffe familiale.

Cadillac
1 to 6 years.
As an aperitif to toast
a new pair of wheels.

Fronsac
4 to 15 years.
Red meat.

Cérons
7 years.
Aperitif, dishes in sauces, desserts.

Côtes de Blaye
6 years.
Seafood

**Côtes
de Bordeaux-Saint-Macaire**
1 to 5 years.
Aperitif.

Côtes de Bourg
A few years.
Red : red meat.
White : white meat.

Côtes de Castillon
4 to 15 years.
Good Saturday night
blow-out.

Entre-Deux-Mers
2 to 4 years.
Products of the seven seas.

Graves
2 to 5 years.
Red : united colours of meat.
White : fish.

Haut-Médoc
5 to 15 years.
Meat.

Lalande-de-Pomerol
4 to 15 years.
Poultry and game.

Listrac-Médoc
5 to 10 years.
Stews and pork.

Loupiac
1 to 10 years.
Roquefort and sorbets.

Lussac-Saint-Emilion
3 to 10 years.
Red meat.

Margaux
5 to 20 years.
Offal, jellied dishes, red meat
in sauce.

Médoc
5 to 10 years.
Country dishes : poultry, rabbit
and cold pork meat.

Montagne-Saint-Emilion
3 to 10 years.
Roast meat.

Moulis
5 to 10 years.
Red meat; stews.

Néac
4 to 15 years.
Poultry and other feathered things.

Pauillac
5 to 20 years.
Red meat and game.

Pessac-Léognan
Rouge : 5 to 10 years.
Blanc : 2 to 6 years.
White : seafood
Red : earthfood.

Pomerol
4 to 20 years.
Poultry and game.

Puisseguin-Saint-Emilion
3 to 15 years.
Meat and game animals.

Saint-Emilion
4 to 25 years.
Roast red meat.

Saint-Estèphe
5 to 15 years.
Confits, cassoulet and siesta.

Saint-Julien
5 to 15 years.
Lamb and fish.

Sainte-Croix-du Mont
1 to 10 years.
Roquefort and sorbet .

Sainte-Foy-Bordeaux
1 to 5 years.
Red : red meat.
White : white fish.

Sauternes
4 to 25 years.
Foie gras and confetti !

WINES OF PROVENCE

note

The note "glug-glug" signifies that the wine should be drunk straight away. (That is one of the undeniable advantagesof rosé, which is drunk young in the summer sun!)

Bandol
Red : 3 to 6 years.
White : 3 years.
Red : stew.
White : bouillabaisses.

Bellet
Red : 3 to 5 years.
Rosé and white : *glug-glug*.
Red : meat.
Rosé and white : home-made salads.

Cassis
Red : 2 to 5 years.
Rosé : *glug-glug*.
Bouillabaisses.

Coteaux Varois
Red : 2 to 4 years.
Rosé : *glug-glug*.
Barbecue party.

Côtes de Provence
Red : 2 to 4 years.
Rosé : 1 to 2 years.
Red : barbecue and roast chicken.
Rosé : fish soup.

Baux-de-Provence
Red : 3 to 5 years.
Rosé : 2 years.
Carnivore menu.

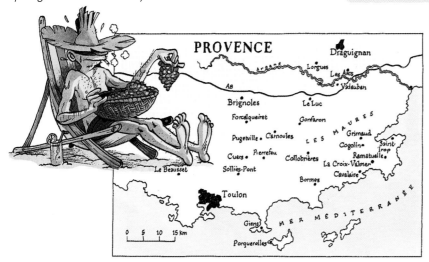

WINES OF THE SOUTH-WEST

Buzet
5 to 10 years
Conserves and cheese, of course.

Cahors
3 to 10 years.
The same.

Côtes de Duras
Red : 5 years.
White : 2 years.
Red : red meat.
White : poached fish.

Côtes du Frontonnais
1 to 3 years.
Goose conserve, casserole, cheese.
(no room for dessert)

Côtes du Marmandais
Red and rosé : 10 years.
White : *glug-glug*.
Red : ewe and goats' cheese
(yeah man!)

Gaillac
Glug-glug.
Red : grilled meat (not burnt)
Rosé and white : endless aperitif.

Vins d'Estaing
Glug-glug.
Family cooking with accordeon
accompaniment.

WINES OF THE PYRÉNÉES

Béarn
Glug-glug.
Dried ham, without sauce.

Irouléguy
2 years.
A gastronomic tour of the Pyrénées:
fine salami, goats cheese,
black cherry conserve,
Bayonne ham.

Jurançon
Dry : *1 to 2 years.*
Mellow : *2 to 8 years.*
Dry : another wine for fans
of smelly cheese.
Mellow : for foie gras blow-outs.

Madiran
1 to 8 years.
Cheese in states of advanced
decomposition.

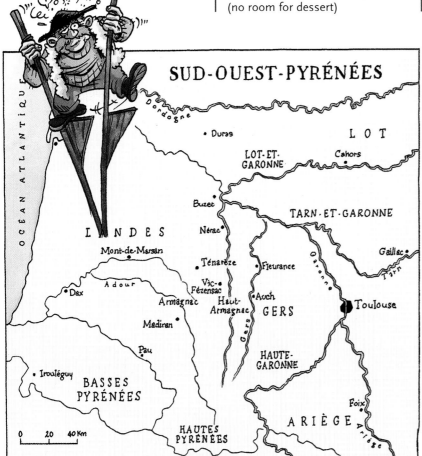

■ WINES OF THE DORDOGNE

Bergerac
Red : *2 to 4 years.*
White and rosé : *glug-glug.*

Côtes de Montravel.
4 years.
Terrines.
Monbazzillac
3 to 20 years
Foie gras or melon
(it all depends on your credit rating).
Montravel
Glug-glug.
Hors-d'œuvre.
Pécharmant
10 years
United colours of barbecue
(More of an ogre's feast than
a princely one).
Rosette
4 years.
Warm starters
(Careful not to be carried out feet
first)
Saussignac
10 years.
Warm starters, fish and desserts.

DORDOGNE

■ WINES OF BURGUNDY

Beaune
2 to 10 years.
Feathered things and jellied blobs.
Bonnes Mares Musigny
4 to 18 years.
Soft veal.
Bourgogne
Glug-glug.
Family blow-out.
Bourgogne Aligoté
Glug-glug.
Eastern European snails.
Bourgogne Passe-Tout-Grains
1 to 2 years.
Coq au vin or bœuf bourgignon
(Obviously!)
Bourgogne-Irancy
2 to 10 years.
Red meat.
Chablis
1 to 15 years.
White meat and cooked ham.
Chambertin
2 to 10 years.
Coq-a-doodle-do au vin.
Chambolle-Musigny
4 to 15 years.
Game.
Charlemagne
5 to 12 years.
Vol au vents and oven-baked tatties.

Chassagne-Montrachet
3 to 10 years.
Red : grilled beef chops.
White : shellfish.
Clos de la Roche
5 to 20 years.
Coq au vin.
Clos de Vougeot
3 to 18 years.
Game.
Clos de Lambrays
5 to 20 years.
Coq au vin.
Clos Saint-Denis
5 to 20 years.
Coq au vin.
(Burgundy is obviously a rotten place
for cockerels!).
Corton
4 to 15 years
Feathered game.
Côte Chalonnaise
Glug-glug.
Family piss-up.
Côte de beaune
2 to 10 years.
Quails and other chicks quite
resigned to losing their feathers.
Crémant de Bourgogne
Glug-glug.
Abundant aperitif.

Echezeaux
5 to 15 years.
Red, white and blue meat.
Fixin
4 to 10 years.
Mutton.
Gevrey-Chambertin
2 to 10 years.
Poultry.
Givry
3 to 10 years.
Carnivore menu.
La Grande Rue
8 to 20 years.
Top-notch cuisine.
(Forget the spaghetti!)
Ladois
2 to 10 years.
Roasted red meat.
Maranges
2 to 8 years.
Another slaughtered cockerel.
Marsannay
5 years.
Roger Rabbit and Bambi.
Mercurey
Red : *3 to 10 years.*
White : *2 to 8 years.*
Isn't bœuf bourgignon a cousin
of the mad cows?

Meursault
2 to 14 years.
Saltwater fish or veal.

Monthélie
3 to 12 years.
Quails and jellied dishes.

Montrachet
12 years.
Top-notch cuisine.

Morey-Saint-Denis
3 to 15 years.
Cooked ham.

Nuits-Saint-Georges
2 to 12 years.
Red meat.

Pommard
3 to 10 years.
Game animals.
(The people of Burgundy certainly
know how to live well!)

Puligny–Montrachet
2 to 8 years.
Veal.

Richebourg
8 to 16 years.
Top-notch cuisine
(Impressive term eh?)

Romanée
8 to 16 years.
Top-notch cuisine
(but what is top-notch cuisine?)

Romannée-Conti
8 to 15 years.
Top-notch cuisine.
(You really want to know?
Alright...a little further on...)

Saint-Aubin
2 to 10 years.
Red meat.

Saint-Romain
3 to 10 years.
Red meat.

Santenay
3 to 10 years.
Sorry, Ladies and Gentlemen,
but we are completely out of cockerel
and beef.

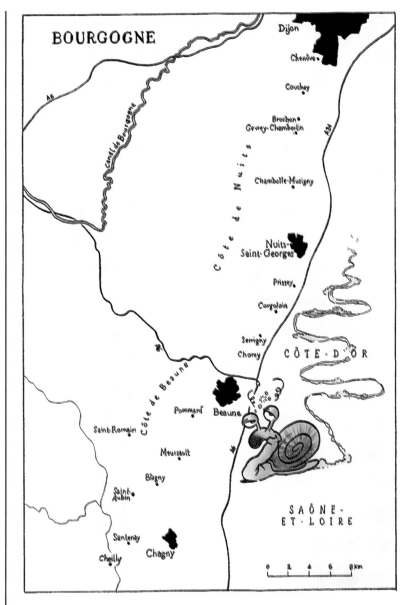

BOURGOGNE

Sauvignon de Saint-Bris
Glug-glug.
Cold ham and salami.

La Tâche
8 to 15 years.
Top-notch cuisine
(but, first of all, what's
your credit-rating like?)

Volnay
2 to 8 years.
Another case for the gamekeepers:
poultry and feathered game.

Vougeot
4 to 16 years.
Same case as above
plus some mutton.

WINES OF BEAUJOLAIS

Beaujolais
1 year
Party till dawn.

Beaujolais-Villages
1 to 4 years.
Family party.

Brouilly
1 to 3 years.
Cholesterol party :
salami.

Chénas
2 to 6 years.
Red meat.

Chiroubles
1 to 3 years.
Family get-together.

Fleurie
18 years.
Game and cheese.

Julienas
1 to 8 years.
Red meat.

Morgon
5 to 12 years.
Red meat, game and cheese.
(and a good siesta!)

Moulin-à-Vent
5 to 10 years.
Same menu as the Morgon.

Régnie
1 to 3 years.
Family piss-up.

Saint-Amour
1 to 5 years.
Wedding anniversary.

WINES OF MACON

Mâcon
1 to 2 years.
Basic cooking.
Pouilly-Fuissé
3 to 10 years.
White and tender meat.
Pouilly-Loché
3 to 8 years.
White and tender meat,
just lightly browned.

Pouilly-Vinzelles
3 to 8 years.
White and tender flesh,
medium browned.
Saint-Veran
2 to 5 years
White and tender flesh,
fully browned.

Château-Grillet
1 to 10 years.
Grilled gratin.
Châteauneuf-du-Pape
Red : *4 to 10 years.*
White : *glug-glug.*
Red : red meat
and game.
White : sun, sea, fish,
shells and shellfish.
Châtillon-en-Dois
Glug-glug.
Family cooking.

Clairette de Die
2 years.
Bring it out with the dessert.
Condrieu
1 to 3 years.
Quenelle.
Cornas
3 to 15 years.
Poultry cooked
in wine.
Côte-Rôtie
5 to 12 years.
Roasted chops.

WINES OF THE RHONES VALLEY

Coteaux du Tricasting
5 years.
Family cooking
Côtes du Luberon
Glug-glug.
White : seaside cuisine.
Red : pool-side cuisine.
Côtes du Ventoux
1 to 4 years.
Red meat.
Côtes-du-rhône
Glug-glug.
Basic family cooking.
Côtes-du-Vivarais.
Glug-glug.
Family cooking.
Crémant de Die
Glug-glug.
Food-less aperitif.
Crozes-Hermitage
Red : *1 to 10 years.*
White : *1 to 5 years.*
Red : pâté.
White : quenelle.

Lirac
Rosé : *1 to 2 years.*
Red : *6 years.*
A bit of fat in the arteries :
cold meat.
Muscat
de Beaumes-de-Venise
Glug-glug.
Sweet for an aperitif.
Bitter for your wallet.
Saint-Joseph
4 to 10 years.
Saint-Joseph wouldn't say
no to some poultry.
Saint-Péray
1 to 10 years.
Advantage :from aperitif to
dessert, by wayof fish in sauce.
Tavel
1 to 5 years.
Grilled fish steak.
Vacqueryas
2 to 6 years.
Marinated meat.

WINES OF LANGUEDOC-ROUSSILLON

Banyuls
3 to 30 years.
Indigestion of the year :
foie gras and chocolate dessert.

Blanquette de Limoux
1 to 2 years.
Consolation menu : almond
biscuits.

Clairette de Bellegarde
1 year.
Local gastronomic stop-off :
brandade de Nîmes (cod).

Collioure
4 to 10 years.
The return of the game animals.

Corbières
2 years.
Classic. Red : meat.
White : fish.

Costières de Nîmes
Glug-glug.
Family cooking.

Côteaux de Languedoc
5 years.
Good food and a few friends.

Côtes de Millau
Glug-glug.
Go straight to the pork-butcher (red)
and to the fishmonger (white).

Cabardès
4 years.
Farting menu : casserole (beans...)

Côtes de Rousillon
Glug-glug.
Family ratatouille.

Faugères
4 to 6 years.
Family knees-up.

Frontignan
1 year.
Leave room for dessert.

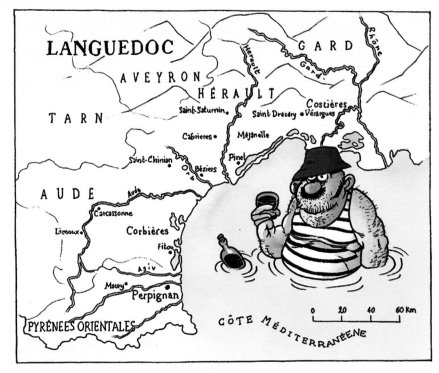

Maury
3 to 20 years.
Smurfs menu :
blue cheese.

Minervois
2 to 4 years.
Grilled fish (white) and
casserole (red).

Muscat de Lunel
1 year.
With or instead of dessert.

Muscat de Mireval
1 year.
Dessert.
(one more for the road).

Muscat de Saint-Jean-de-Minervois
1 year.
Smurf menu : blue
ewe cheese.

Rivesaltes
Glug-glug.
No alibi needed : afternoon wine!

Saint-Chinian
4 to 6 years.
All-rounder :
meat, poultry, cheese...

WINES FROM THE LOIRE AND ANJOU

Anjou
Dry white : *2 to 3 years.*
Mellow white : *3 to 6 years.*
Red : *4 to 6 years.*
Cheerful menus :
meat and goats cheese
(red), shellfish and
fried fish (dry white),
fish in sauce
(mellow white).

Anjou Gamay
Glug-glug.
All meat, feathered or not.

Bonnezeaux
40 years.
Special occasions.
Foie gras and poached poultry.

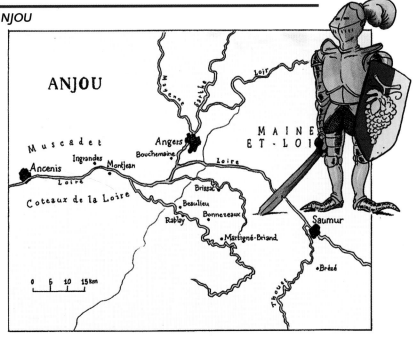

Bourgueil
Saint-Nicolas-de-Bourgueil
River-terrace wine : *2 to 4 years.*
Hillside wine : *20 years.*
Stuff-your-face menu :
meat in wine sauce, cheese.

Cabernet d'Anjou
4 years.
Return of The Cholesterol :
cold ham and salami.

Cabernet de Saumur
4 years
Revenge of The Cholesterol :
cold ham and meat.

Cheverny
Glug-glug.
Home cooking.

Chinon
River-terrace wine : *2 to 4 years.*
Hillside wine : *25 years.*
Gargantuan menu :
roast red meat,
meat in wine sauce, game,
cheese.

Côteau de Saumur
4 years.
Hot menu :
baked andouillette (sausage).

Côteau du Loir
Glug-glug.
Red : potted meat.
White : white pudding.

Coteaux d'Ancenis
Glug-glug.
I only accept cold ham and salami.

Coteaux du Layon
10 to 30 years.
Slimming menu : foie gras.

Côtes de Gien
Glug-glug.
Family cooking.

Gros Plant du Pays Nantais
2 years.
Good stuff : seafood
and fatty fish.

Jasnières
10 years.
Goat's cheese.

Montlouis
5 to 10 years.
Ewe cheese.

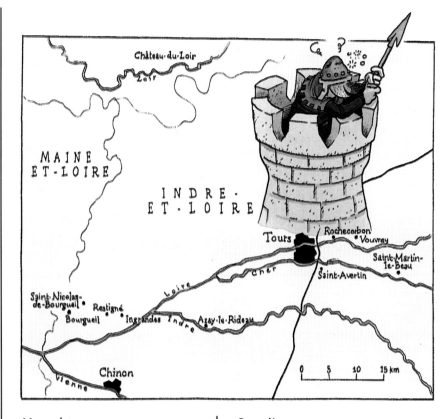

Muscadet
Glug-glug
Without alibi : at the bar.
With alibi : at table with fish.

Muscadet de Sèvre-et-Maine
5 years.
Shellfish.

Rosé d'Anjou
1 year.
Red meat and white meat
for this rosé.

Rosé de Loire
1 year.
Family cooking.

Saumur
4 years.
Not for those on a diet :
cold ham and salami,
fried fish (white)
meat and poultry (red).

Saumur-Champigny
2 to 4 years.
Grills and roasts.

Savenières
20 to 30 years.
Fisherman's menu : fish
and shellfish in sauce, siesta.

Touraine
Glug-glug.
United Colours of Wine menu :
Cold ham and salami (rosé),
freshwater fish (white),
game (red),
vomit (multi-coloured).

Touraine-Azay-le-Rideau
Glug-glug.
Open the family freezer.

Vouvray
5 to 15 years.
Dry : cold ham/salami,
poultry, fish.
Soft and fizzy : aperitif,
dessert, aspirin.

■ WINES FROM THE CENTRE

Pouilly Fumé
2 to 8 years
Slimming menu :
fish and cheese.

Saint-Pourçain
Glug-glug.
100% family cuisine.

Sancerre
2 to 8 years
Red : meat.
White : fish.

Alsace-Grand-Cru
20 years.
"Intro" menu : foie gras as aperitif.
Crémant d'Alsace
Glug-glug.
"Stuff yourself and get pissed
before the meal" menu :
aperitif with foie gras.
Gewurtztraminerg
1 to 15 years.
Bretzel and Kouglof.
Moselle
1 year.
"Armoured stomach" menu:
shellfish and cold ham/salami.
Muscat
4 years
Diabetes menu :
desserts and pâtisseries.
Pinot noir
5 years.
Sauerkraut with meat.
Riesling
2 to 6 years.
Revenge of Sauerkraut.
Sylvaner
1 to 2 years.
Bride of Sauerkraut.
Tokay
2 to 15 years.
It' OK for fish in sauce.

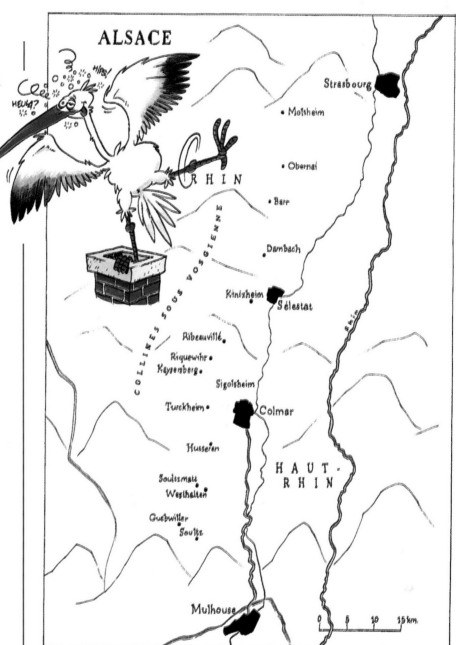

Achevé d'imprimer sur les presses de Pozzo Gross Monti, CEE.